THE KIDS' BOOK OF DOT TO DOT 1

Puzzles by
Emily Golden Twomey

Buster Books

Contents

Introduction

A challenging collection of connect-the-dot puzzles to discover and colour.

The puzzles come in four levels of difficulty – with Beginners, Intermediates and Advanced and then the ultimate challenge, Ace Puzzlers. The number of dots to connect range from 20 to over 100. Some pictures contain more than one puzzle challenge.

The answers are at the back if you get lost and need to take a sneak peak to get back on track.

Level One:
Beginners

Puzzle 1

Puzzle 3

Puzzle 4

Puzzle 6

Puzzle 7

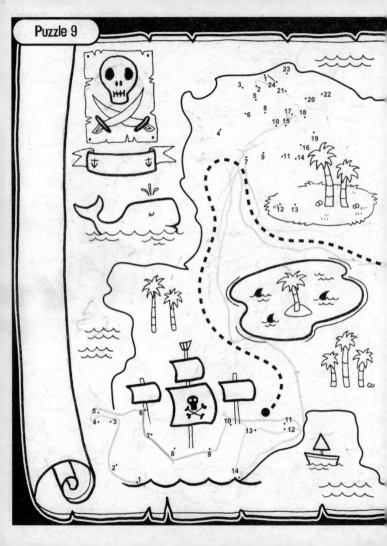

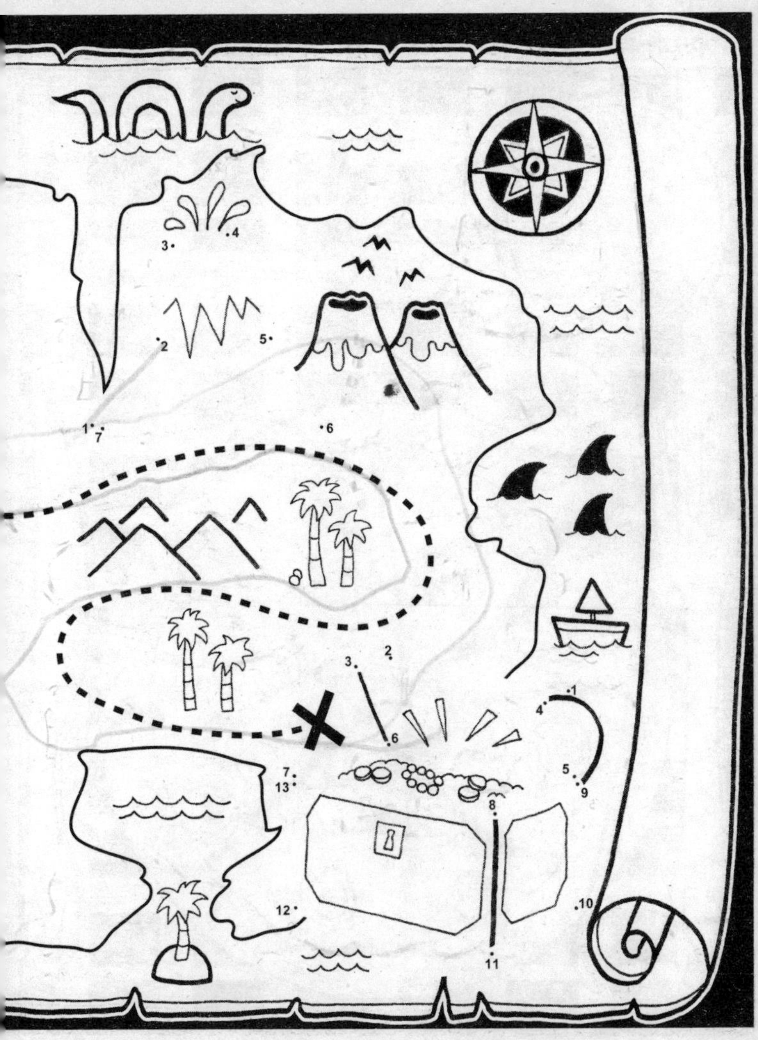

Puzzle 10

Puzzle 12

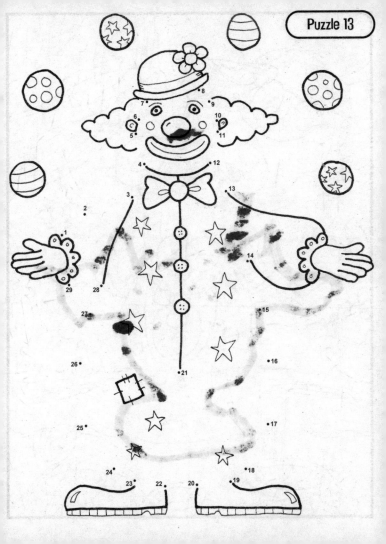

Puzzle 13

Puzzle 14

Puzzle 15

Puzzle 16

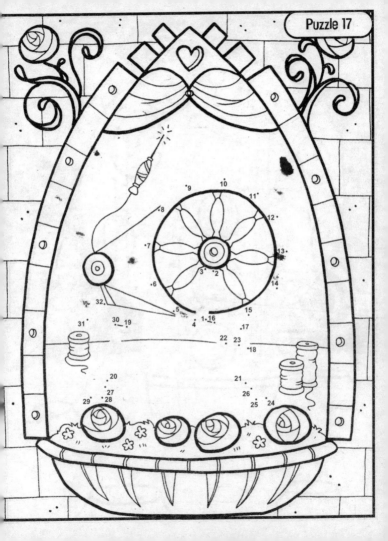

Puzzle 18

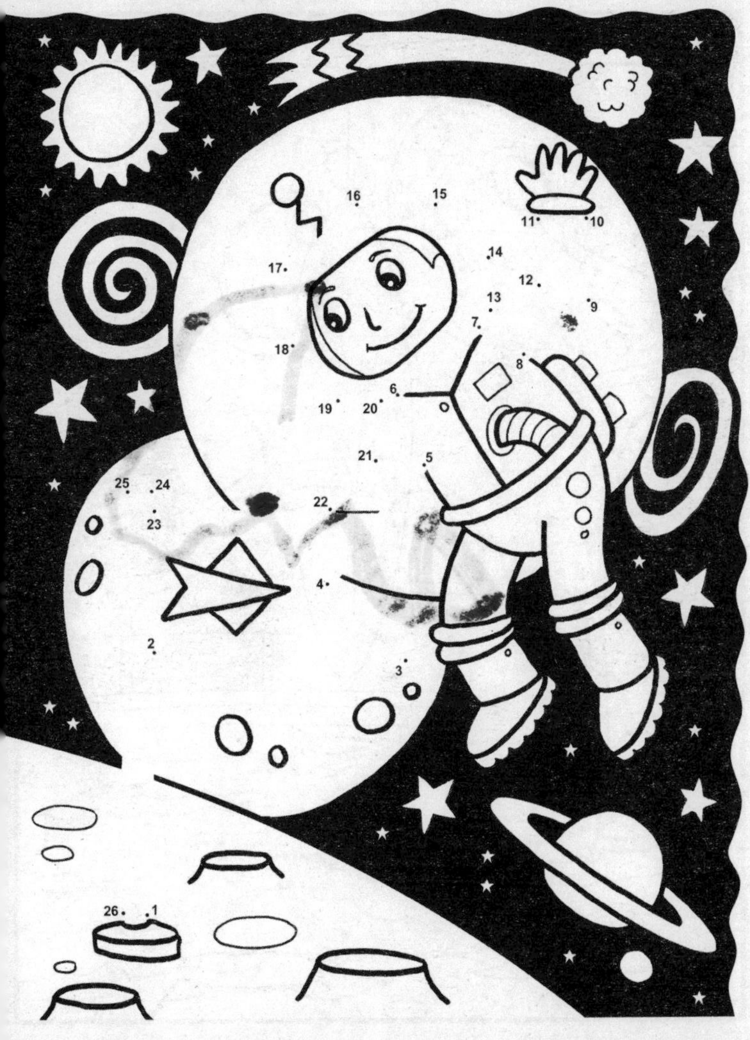
16
15
11
10
14
17
12
13
9
7
18
8
6
19
20
21
5
25
24
23
22
4
2
3
26
1

Puzzle 19

Puzzle 21

Puzzle 22

Puzzle 23

Puzzle 24

Puzzle 25

Puzzle 26

1
2
3
4
5
6
7
8
9
10
11
12
13
14
15
16
17
18
19
20
21
22
23
24
25
26
27
28
29
30
31
32
33
34
35
36
37
38
39
40
41
42
43
44

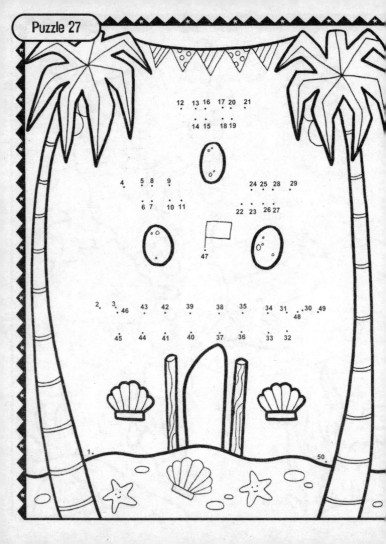

Puzzle 28

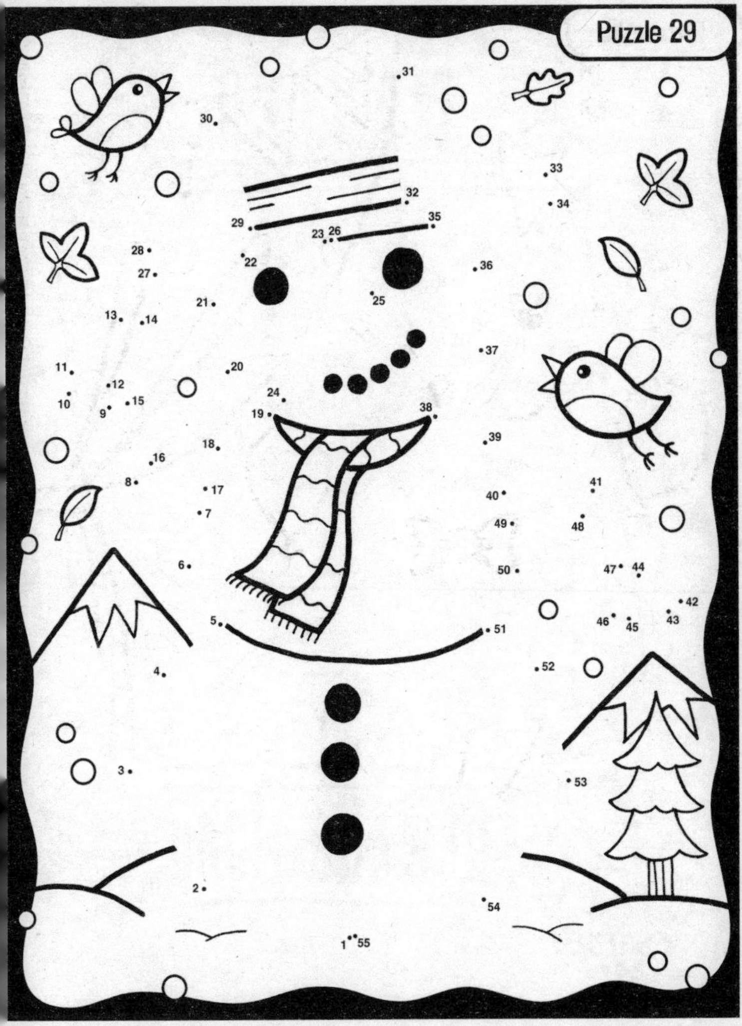
Puzzle 29

Puzzle 31

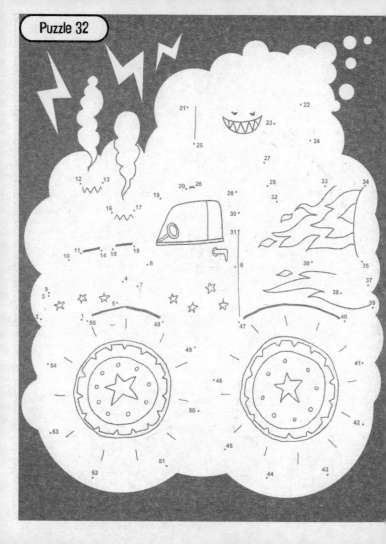

Puzzle 34

Level Two:
Intermediates

Puzzle 36

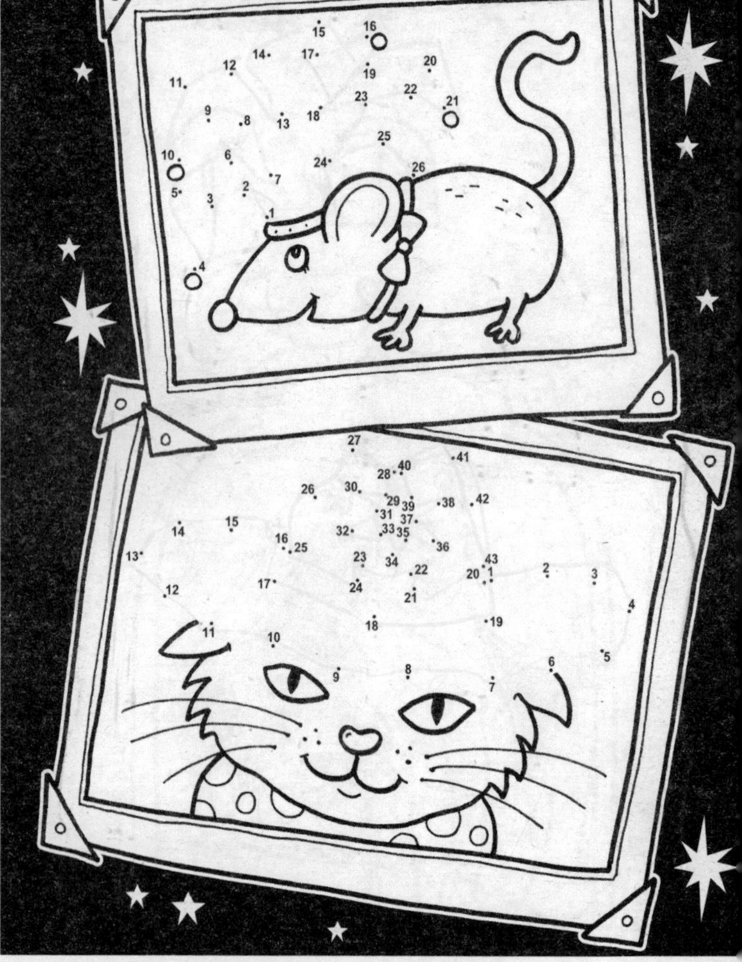

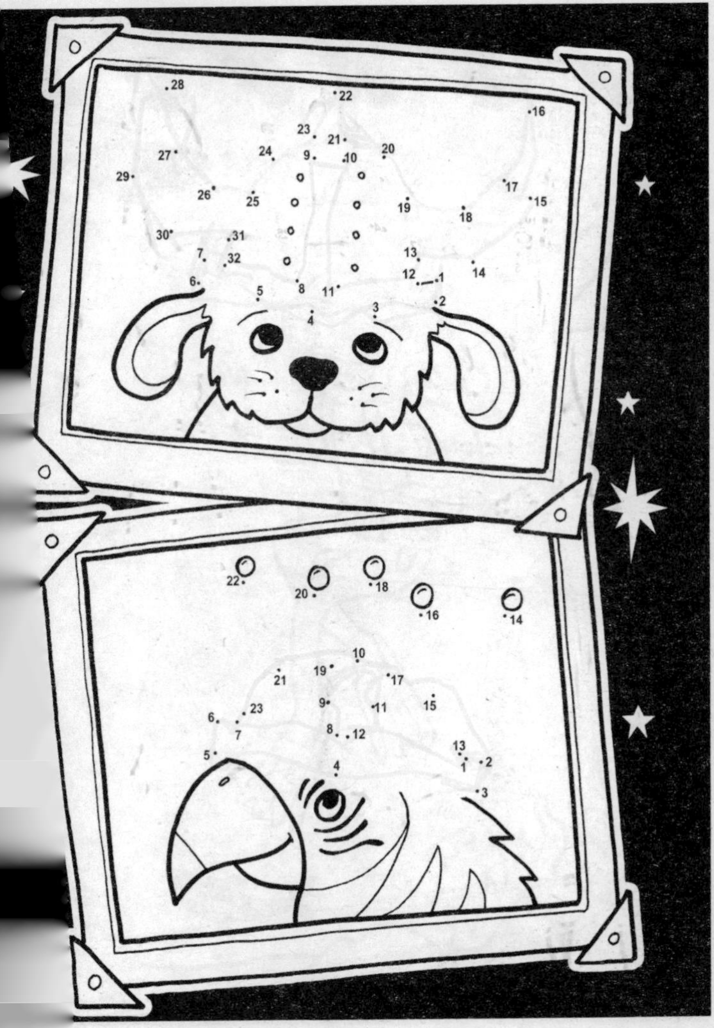

Puzzle 37

Puzzle 38

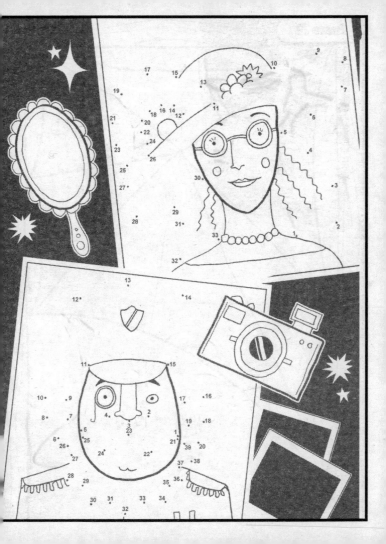

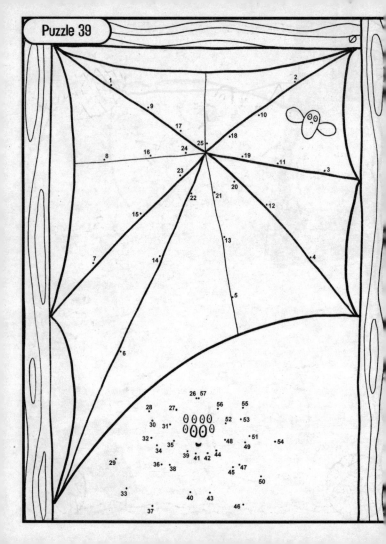

Puzzle 40

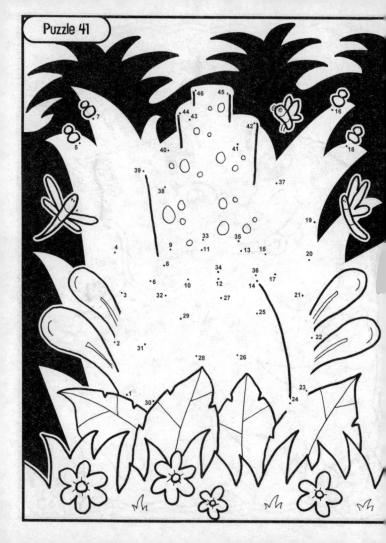

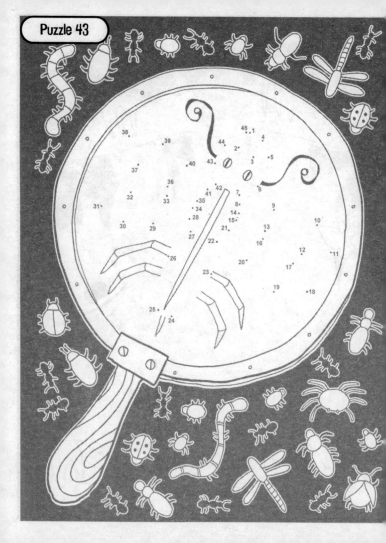

Puzzle 43

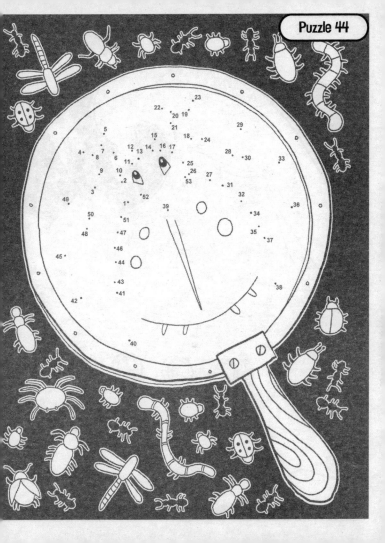

Puzzle 45

Puzzle 46

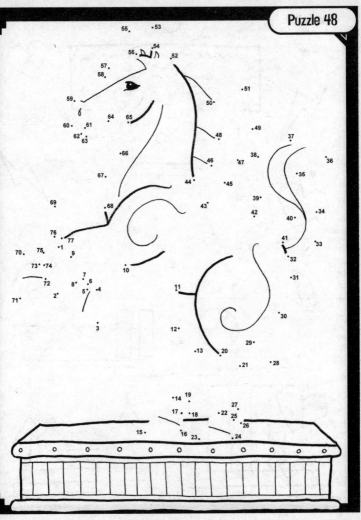

Puzzle 50

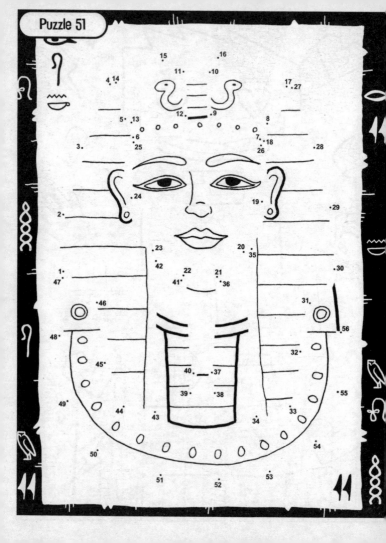

Puzzle 51

Puzzle 52

Puzzle 53

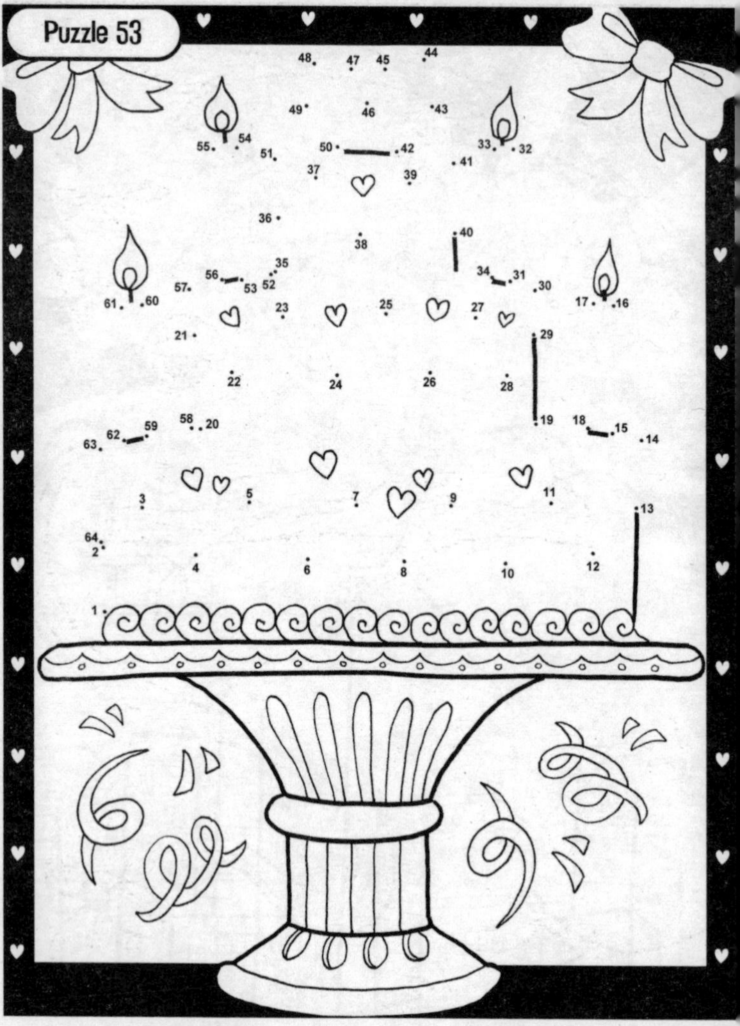

Puzzle 54

Puzzle 55

64 · · 60 · 59 · 56 · · 55
· 63

66 · 65 · 62 — 61 · 58 — 57 · — 54 · 53

43 · 45 · 49 · 51

42 ·

44 · 50 · 52

68 · 67 · 41 · 46 · 48 · 47 · 40

31 · 32 · 34 · 36 · 38

33 · 35 · 37 · 39

70 · 69 · 30 · 29

19 · 21 · 23 · 25 · 26 · 28 · 11

20 · 22 · 24 · 27

17 · 15 · 13 · 18 · 12

18 · 4 · 16 · 6 · 14 · 8 · 10

3 · 5 · 7 · 9 · 1

2 · 1

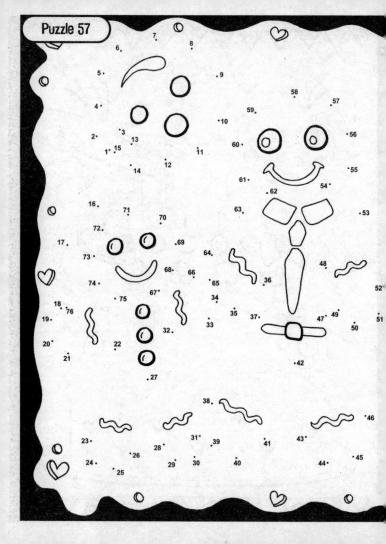

Puzzle 57

Puzzle 58

Puzzle 59

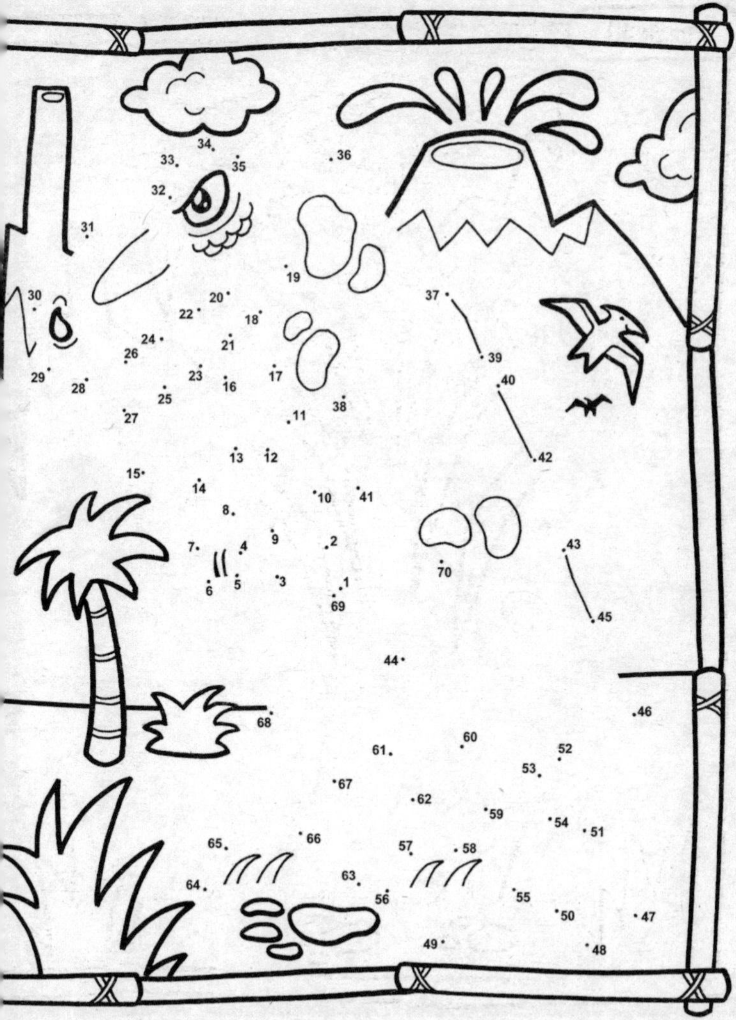

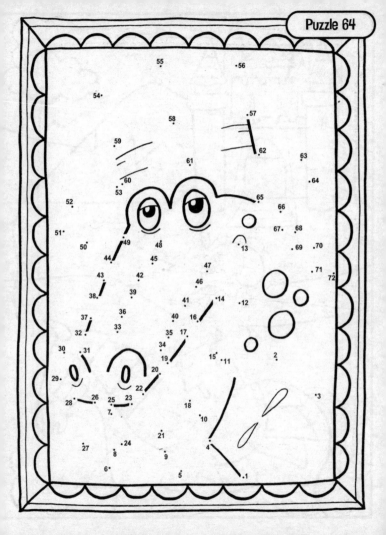

Puzzle 64

Puzzle 65

Puzzle 67

Puzzle 69

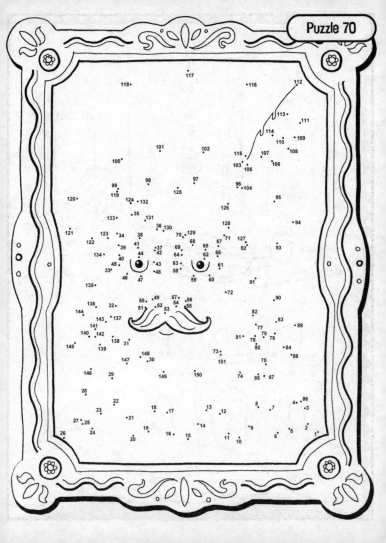

Puzzle 71

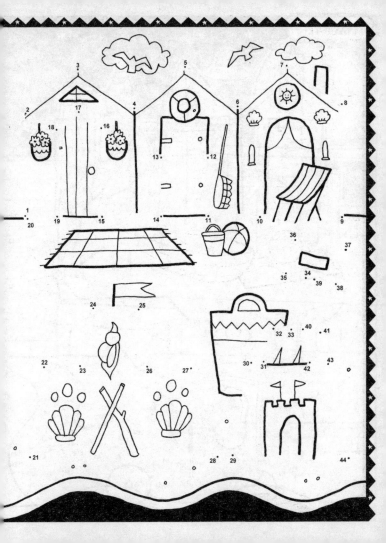

Puzzle 72

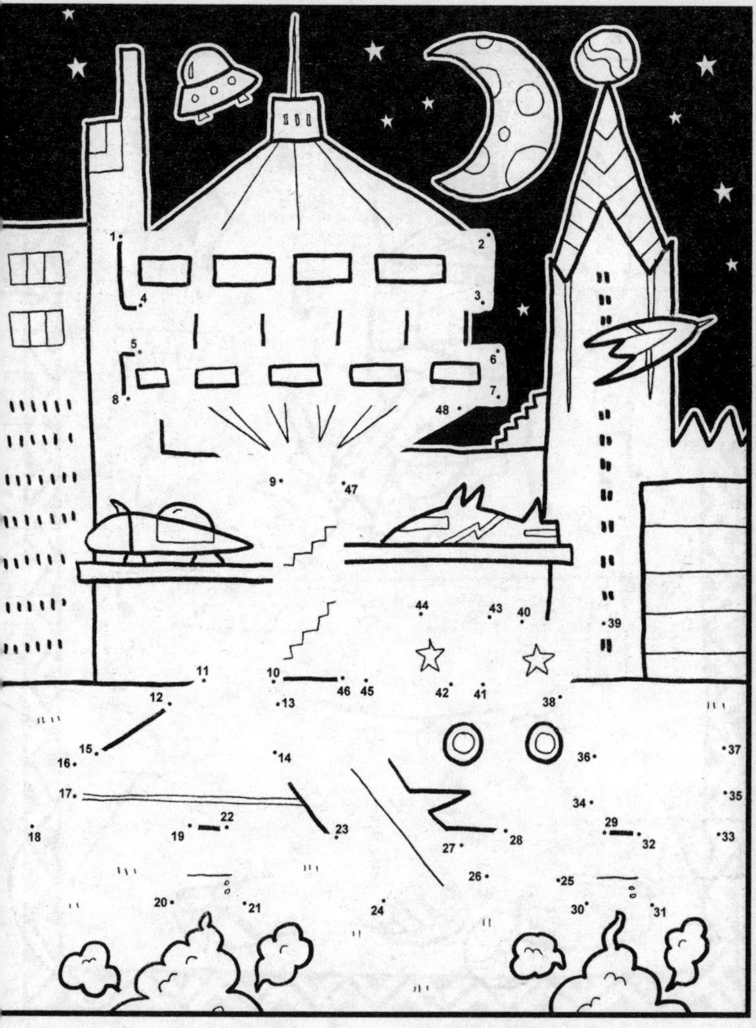

Puzzle 77

Puzzle 78

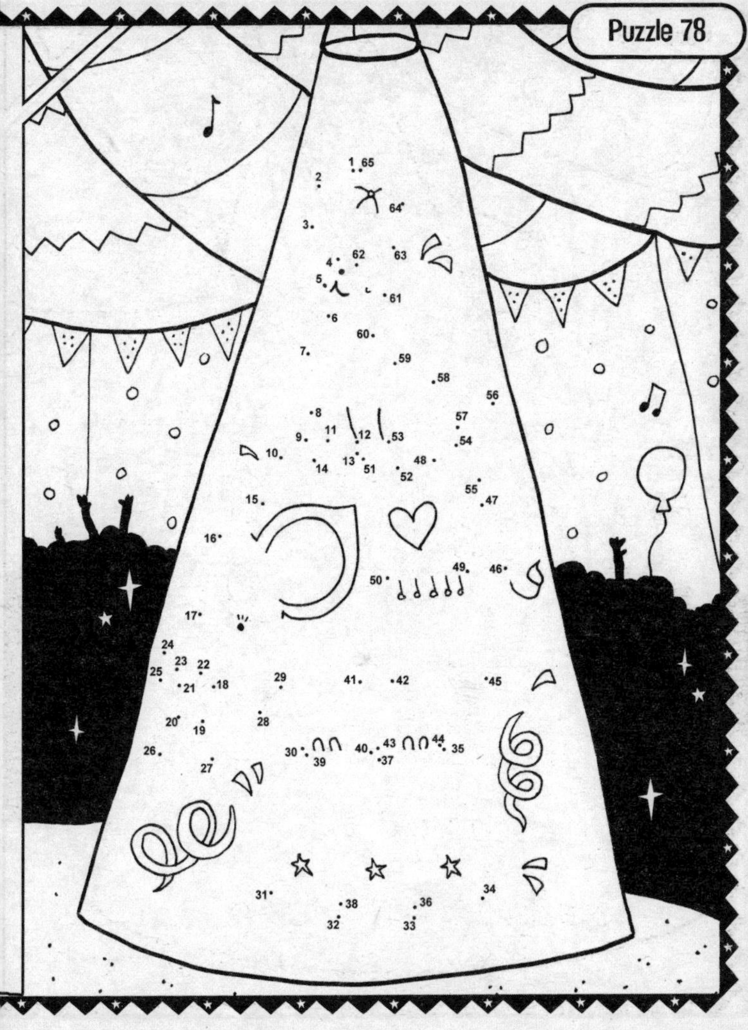

Puzzle 79

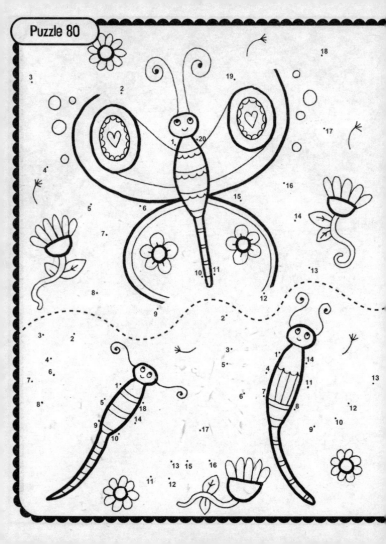

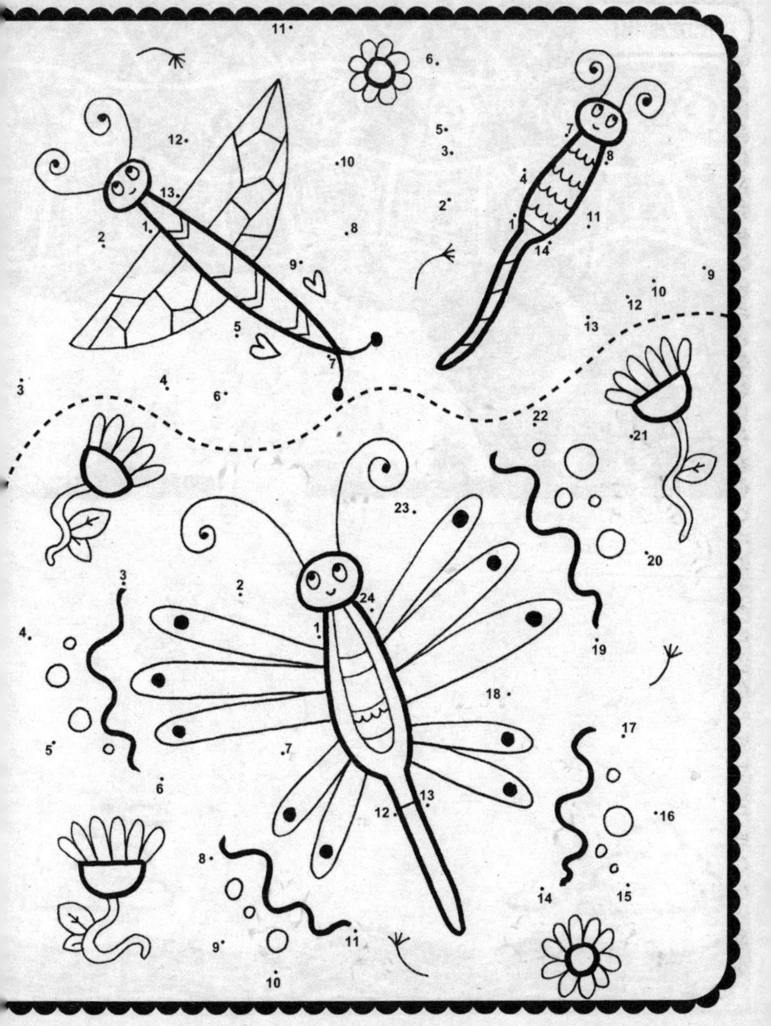

Puzzle 81

Puzzle 82

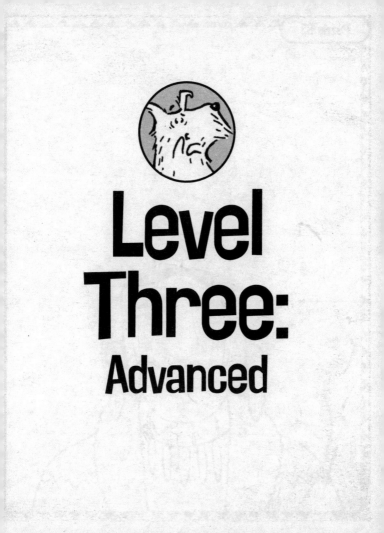

Level
Three:
Advanced

Puzzle 84

Puzzle 85

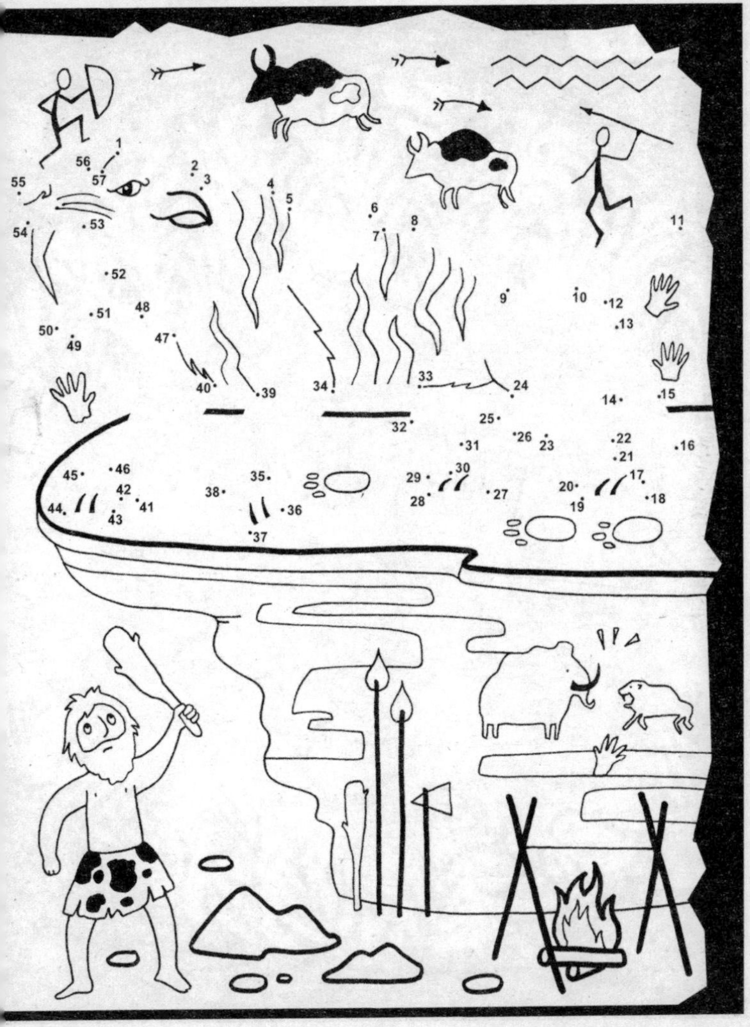

Puzzle 87

1
2
3
4
5
6
7
8
9
10
11
12
13
14
15
16
17
18
19
20
21
22
23
24
25
26
27
28
29
30
31
32
33
34
35
36
37
38
39
40
41
42
43
44
45
46
47
48
49
50
51
52
53
54

Puzzle 88

Puzzle 89

Puzzle 92

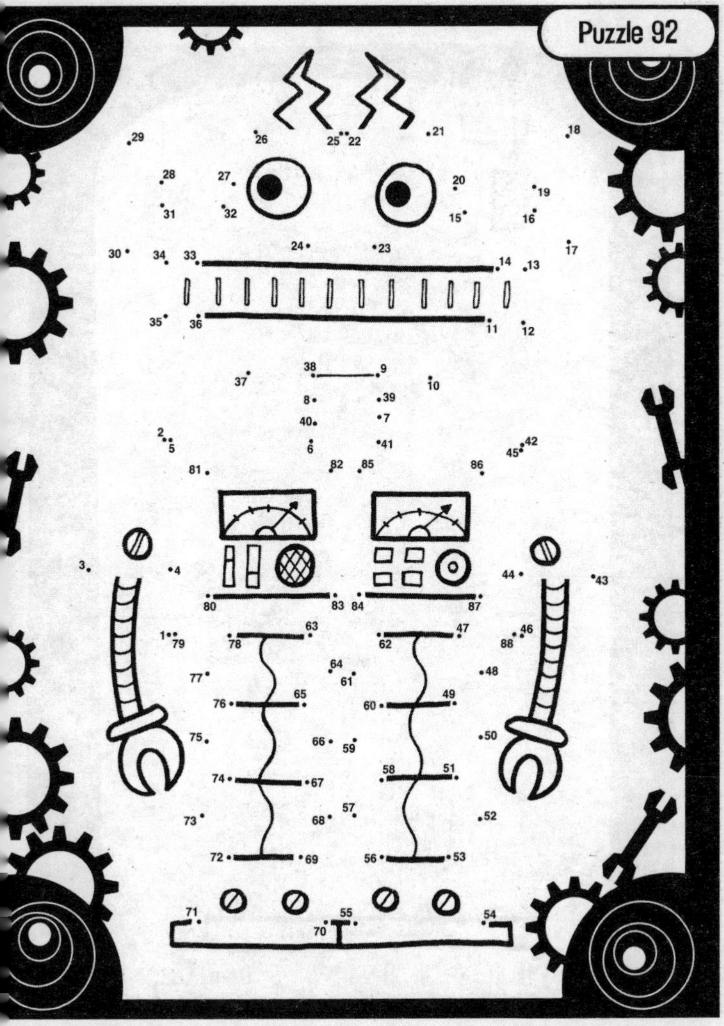

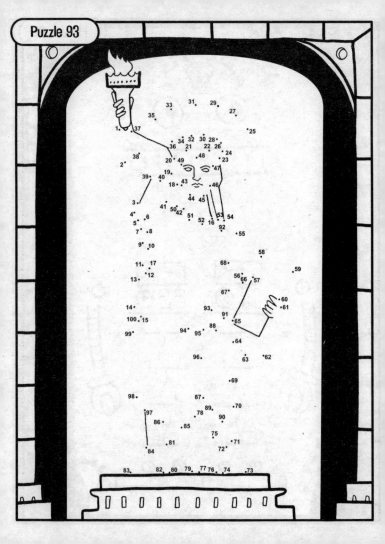

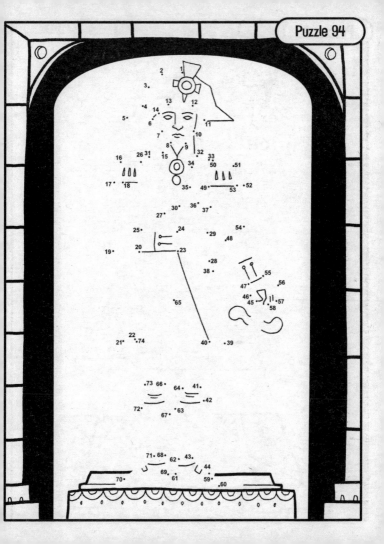

Puzzle 94

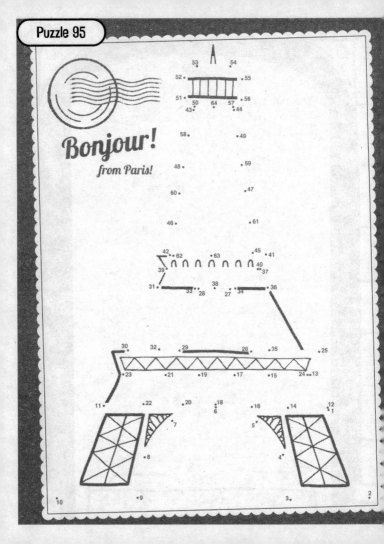

Puzzle 95

Bonjour!
from Paris!

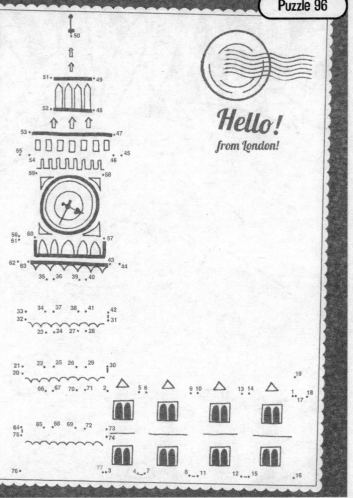

Hello!
from London!

Puzzle 97

Puzzle 98

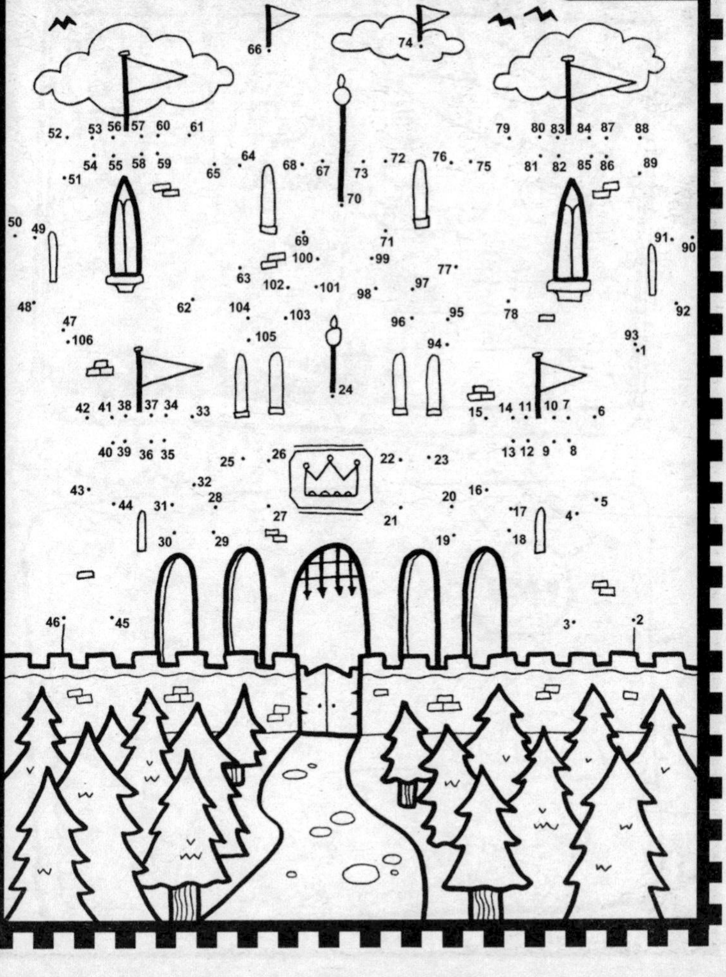

Puzzle 99

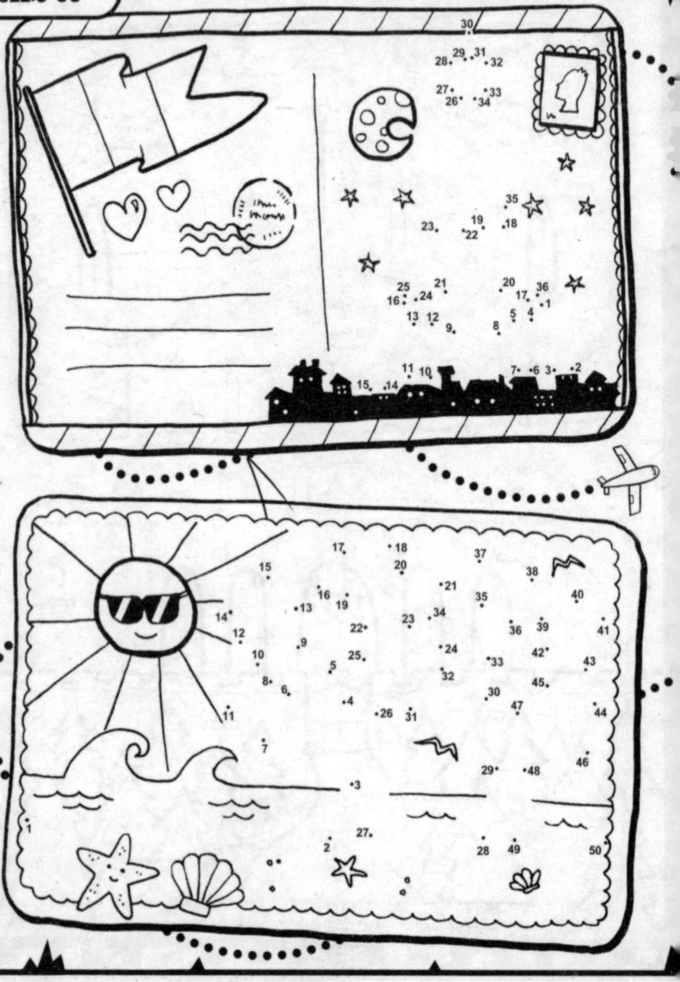

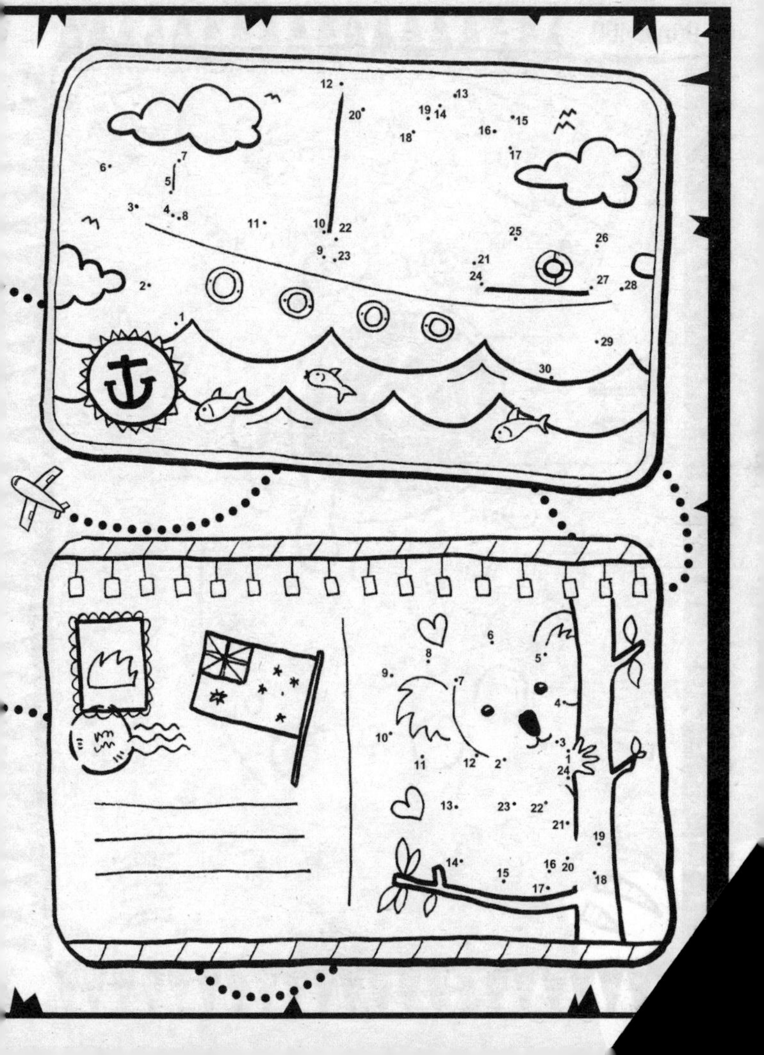

Puzzle 100

1
2
3
4
5
6
7
8
9
10
11
12
13
14
15
16
17
18
19
20
21
22
23
24
25
26
27
28
29
30
31
32
33
34
35
36
37
38
39
40
41
42
43
44
45
46
47
48
49
50
51
52
53
54
55
56
57
58
59
60
61
62
63
64
65
66
67
68
69
70
71
72
73
4
75
76
77
78
79
80
81
82
83
84
85
86
87
88
89
90
91
92
93

Puzzle 101

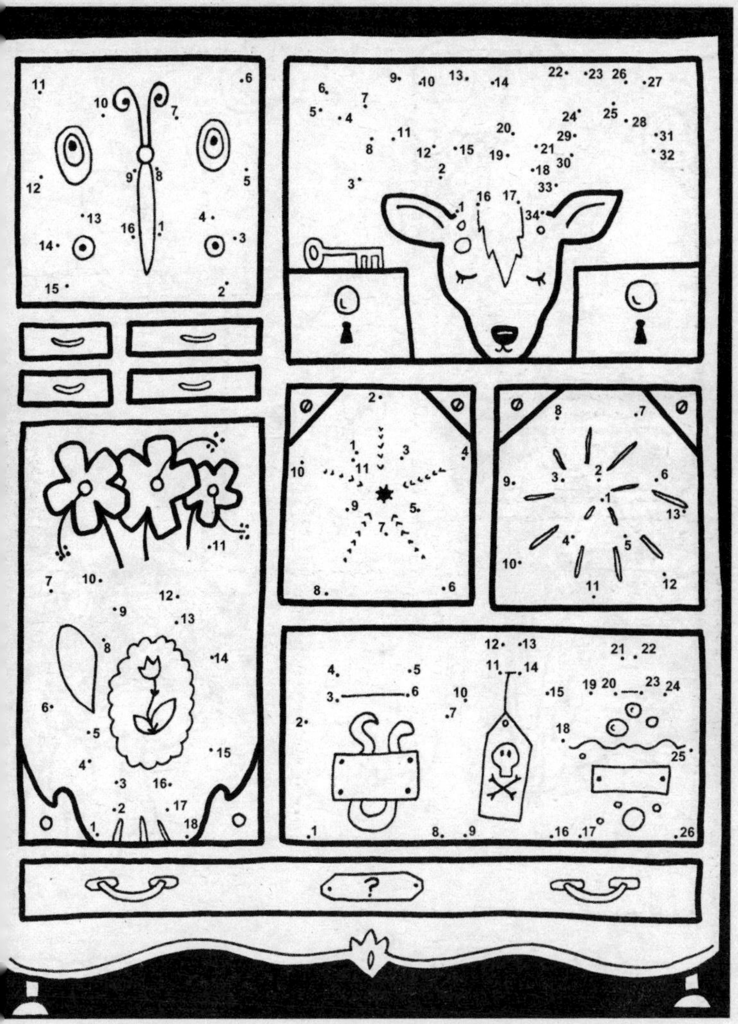

Puzzle 103

1
2
3
4
5
6
7
8
9
10
11
12
13
14
15
16
17
18
19
20
21
22
23
24
25
26
27
28
29
30
31
32
33
34
35
36
37
38
39
40
41
42
43
44
45
46
47
48
49
50
51
52
53
54
55

Puzzle 104

Puzzle 105

Puzzle 108

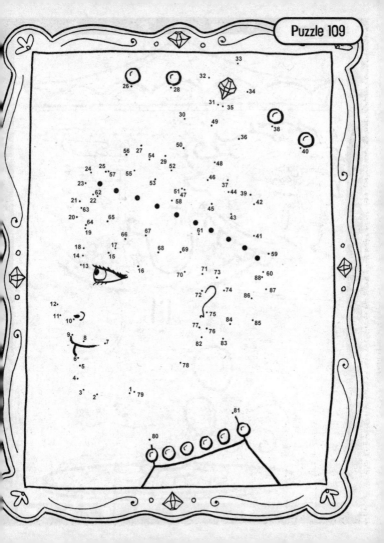

Puzzle 110

Puzzle 111

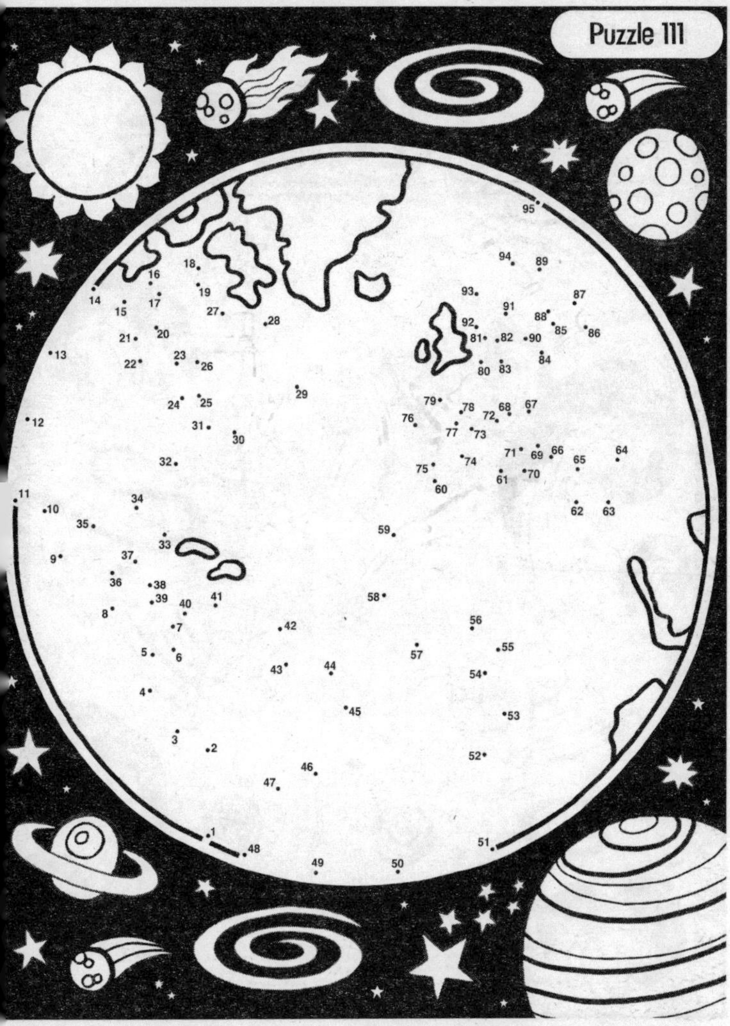
1
2
3
4
5
6
7
8
9
10
11
12
13
14
15
16
17
18
19
20
21
22
23
24
25
26
27
28
29
30
31
32
33
34
35
36
37
38
39
40
41
42
43
44
45
46
47
48
49
50
51
52
53
54
55
56
57
58
59
60
61
62
63
64
65
66
67
68
69
70
71
72
73
74
75
76
77
78
79
80
81
82
83
84
85
86
87
88
89
90
91
92
93
94
95

Level Four:
Ace Puzzlers

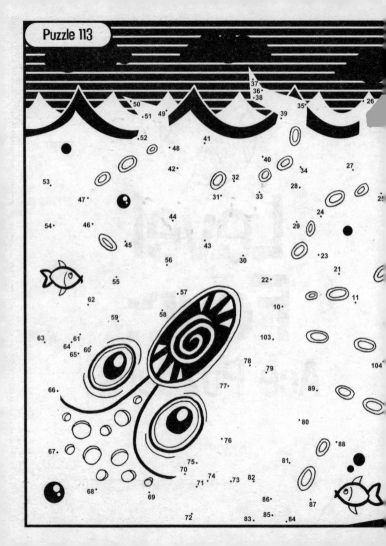

Puzzle 113

Puzzle 114

Puzzle 115

Puzzle 116

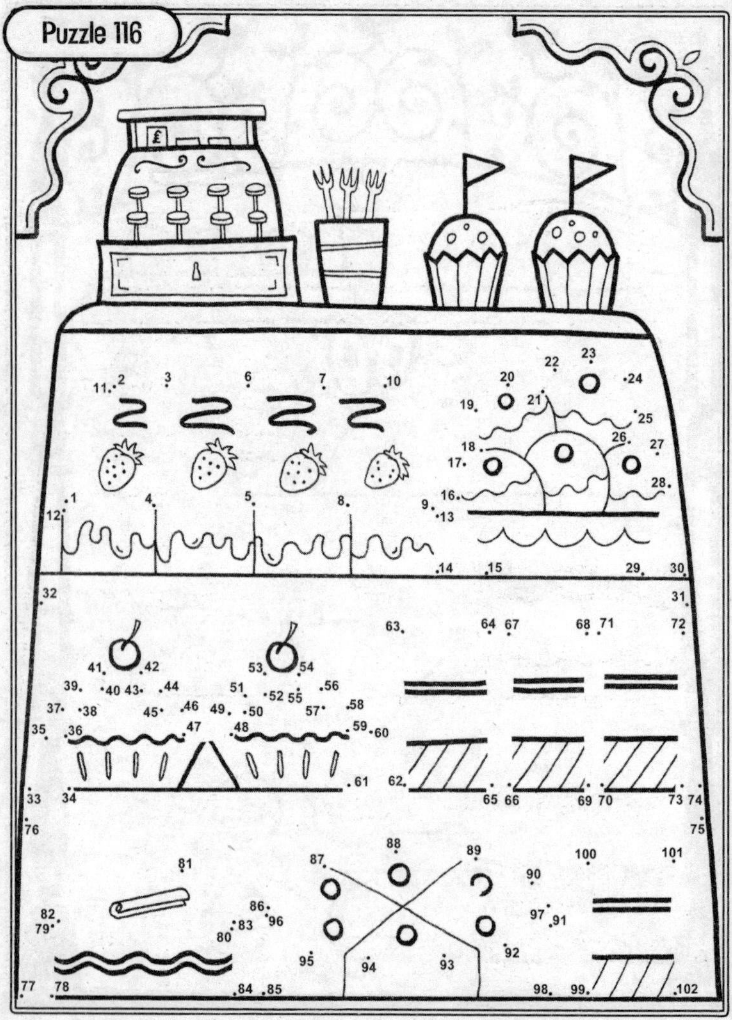
£
1
2
3
4
5
6
7
8
9
10
11
12
13
14
15
16
17
18
19
20
21
22
23
24
25
26
27
28
29
30
31
32
33
34
35
36
37
38
39
40
41
42
43
44
45
46
47
48
49
50
51
52
53
54
55
56
57
58
59
60
61
62
63
64
65
66
67
68
69
70
71
72
73
74
75
76
77
78
79
80
81
82
83
84
85
86
87
88
89
90
91
92
93
94
95
96
97
98
99
100
101
102

Puzzle 117

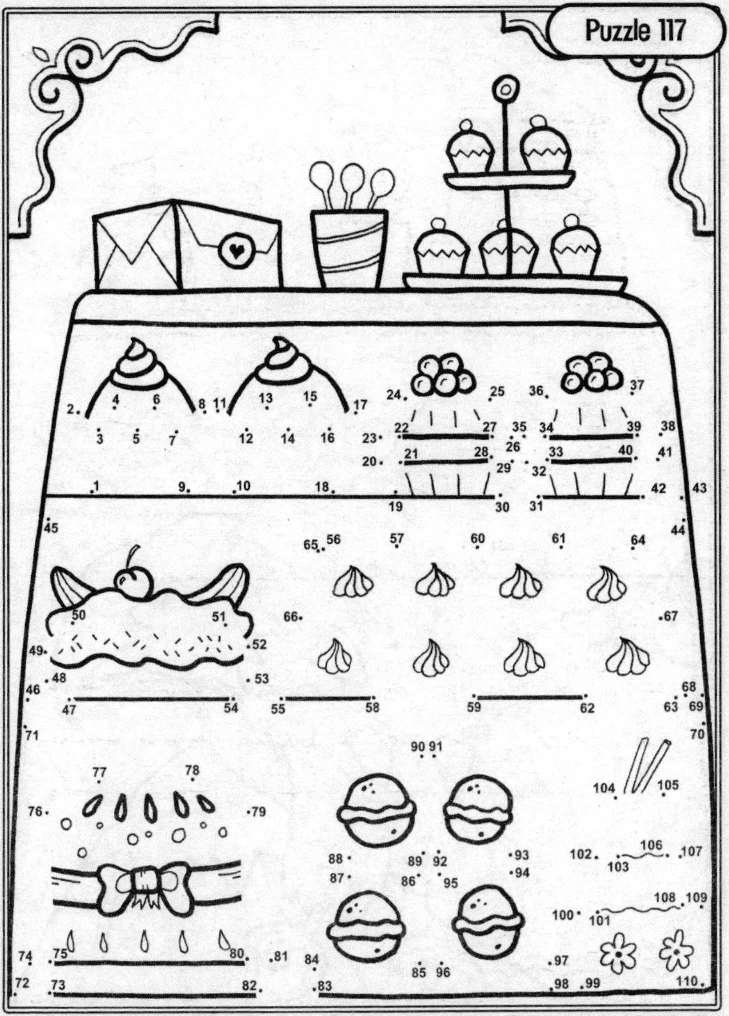

Puzzle 118

Puzzle 120

Puzzle 121

Answers

Puzzle 1

Puzzle 2

Beginners

Puzzle 3

Puzzle 4

Puzzle 5

Puzzle 6

Puzzle 7

Puzzle 8

Puzzle 9

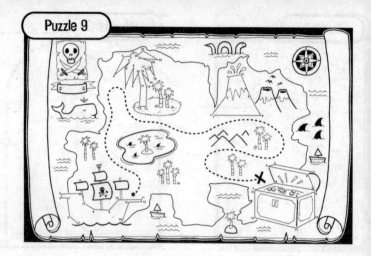

Puzzle 10

Puzzle 11

Puzzle 16

Puzzle 17

Puzzle 18

Puzzle 19

Puzzle 20

Puzzle 21

Puzzle 22

Puzzle 23

Puzzle 24

Puzzle 25

Puzzle 26

Puzzle 27

Puzzle 28

Puzzle 29

Puzzle 30

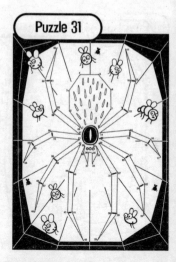

Puzzle 31

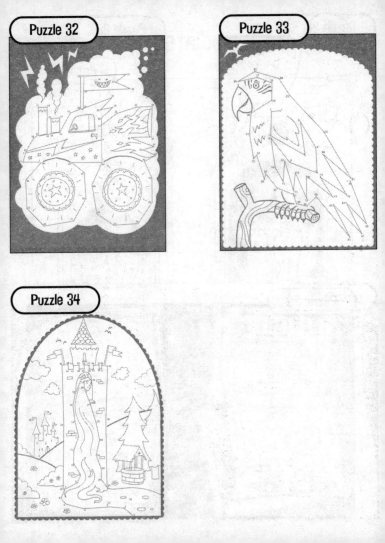

Puzzle 32

Puzzle 33

Puzzle 34

Intermediates

Puzzle 37

Puzzle 38

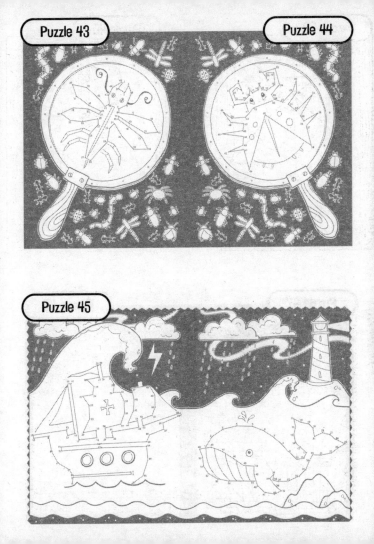

Puzzle 46

Puzzle 47

Puzzle 48

Puzzle 49

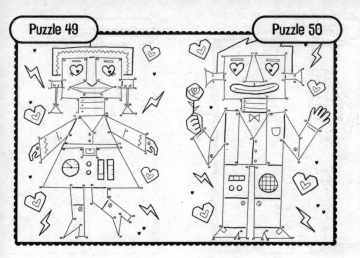

Puzzle 50

Puzzle 51

Puzzle 52

Puzzle 53

Puzzle 54

Puzzle 55

Puzzle 56

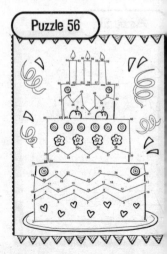

Puzzle 57

Puzzle 58

Puzzle 59

Puzzle 60

Puzzle 61

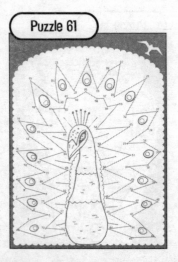

Puzzle 62

Puzzle 63

Puzzle 64

Puzzle 65

Puzzle 66

Puzzle 67

Puzzle 68

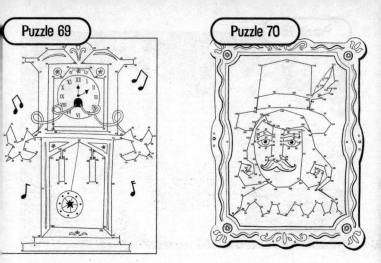

Puzzle 69

Puzzle 70

Puzzle 71

Puzzle 72

Puzzle 73

Puzzle 74

Puzzle 79

Puzzle 80

Puzzle 81

Puzzle 82

Puzzle 86

Puzzle 87

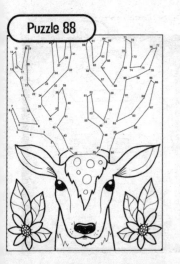

Puzzle 88

Puzzle 89

Puzzle 90

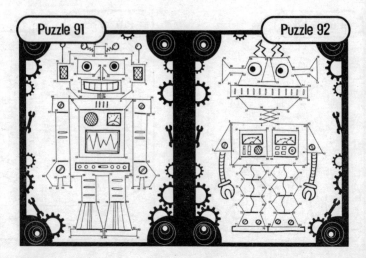

Puzzle 91

Puzzle 92

Puzzle 93

Puzzle 94

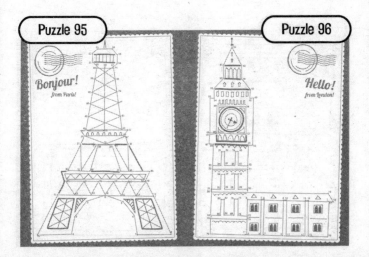

Puzzle 95

Bonjour!
from Paris!

Puzzle 96

Hello!
from London!

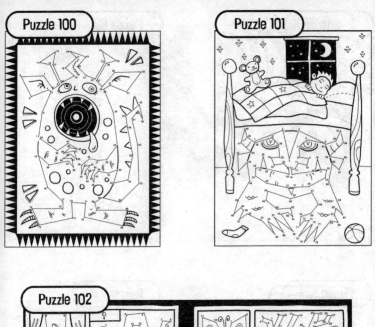

Puzzle 100

Puzzle 101

Puzzle 102

Puzzle 103

Puzzle 104

Puzzle 105

Puzzle 106

Puzzle 107

Puzzle 108

Puzzle 109

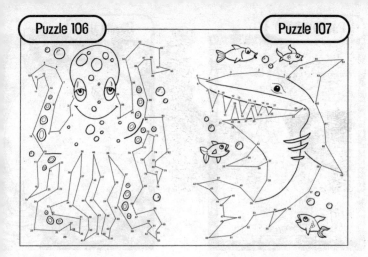

Puzzle 110

Puzzle 111

Puzzle 112

Ace Puzzlers

Puzzle 113

Puzzle 114

Puzzle 115

Puzzle 116

Puzzle 117

Puzzle 118

Puzzle 119

Revised paperback edition first published in 2017

First published in Great Britain in 2015 by Buster Books,
an imprint of Michael O'Mara Books Limited,
9 Lion Yard, Tremadoc Road, London SW4 7NQ

 www.mombooks.com/buster   Buster Books   @BusterBooks   @Buster_Books

This book contains material previously published in *The Kids' Book of Dot to Dot*,
Dot To Dot and *Buster's Brilliant Dot To Dot*.

Puzzles by Emily Golden Twomey
Illustrations by John Bigwood
Edited by Sophie Schrey and Philippa Wingate

A CIP catalogue record for this book is available from the British Library.

ISBN: 978-1-78055-505-8

5 7 9 10 8 6

Papers used by Buster Books are natural, recyclable products made of wood from
well-managed, FSC®-certified forests and other controlled sources. The manufacturing
processes conform to the environmental regulations of the country of origin.

Layout designed by Zoe Bradley

Printed and bound in November 2020 by CPI Group (UK) Ltd,
108 Beddington Lane, Croydon, CR0 4YY, United Kingdom

MIX
Paper from
responsible sources
FSC® C020471
www.fsc.org

Also Available:

The Kids' Book
of Puzzles 1

ISBN: 978-1-78055-504-1   £3.99

THE KIDS'
BOOK OF
PUZZLES 1

OVER
100
puzzles